The FASB Cases on Recognition and Measurement

Edited by
L. Todd Johnson

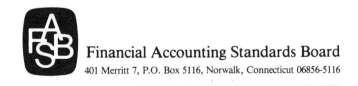

Financial Accounting Standards Board
401 Merritt 7, P.O. Box 5116, Norwalk, Connecticut 06856-5116

IRWIN 1991, Homewood, Illinois 60430

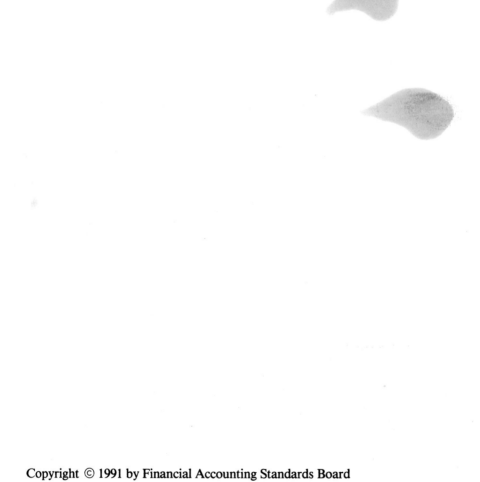

FOREWORD

Recognition and measurement issues are pervasive. Questions about when to recognize and how to measure assets, liabilities, revenues, and expenses are at the heart of most of the real accounting issues that are or have been on the agenda of the Financial Accounting Standards Board and its predecessors.

This casebook has its roots in the FASB's conceptual framework project, and many of the cases were originally prepared as part of the recognition and measurement phase of that project. The cases helped the Board and staff focus on certain conceptual issues and facilitated communication between the Board and staff about those issues. The cases helped identify and clarify many questions, sharpening the focus on the concepts underlying them. In some instances, the cases helped overcome perceived differences of opinion, while in others, they revealed previously hidden ones. In either event, they helped advance the dialogue and ultimately the project itself.

When the recognition and measurement phase of the project was concluded, the cases were consigned to the FASB's files, along with other materials germane to the project. Having served their purpose, they were thought to be of little further interest. However, that proved to be untrue. In considering later agenda projects, the Board and staff found the cases kept coming up as useful in providing contexts for analyzing the issues inherent in current topics. Analogies were drawn between agenda items and individual cases, as the issues embodied in some of the cases turned out to be the same as those in agenda projects. The issues in the cases also were identified in some of the issues being considered by the FASB's Emerging Issues Task Force (EITF).

Clearly, the cases had developed a life of their own. Because they proved so valuable to us, the idea emerged that others might find them to be valuable as well, and we decided to share them with others by publishing this book. Although the casebook is unique among FASB publications, it is consistent with the educational aspect of the FASB's mission, which is to improve the common understanding of the nature and purposes of information contained in financial reports.

This collection is not intended to represent a comprehensive or exhaustive survey of conceptual issues in accounting. Rather, it represents a cross section that the Board and staff have found useful over the years in discussing conceptual matters in recognition and measurement. A few cases originated from internal discussions of issues related to other projects, and the remainder were prepared specifically for this book to round out the collection.

Although some of the situations in the cases are addressed in the authoritative literature, the cases are intended to raise conceptual issues for which there are no "right" answers. The cases provide a means for comparing and contrasting a variety of positions that can be taken on the issues. Because there are no right answers, there is no "solutions manual" that accompanies the casebook. However, a separate Discussion Guide is available to instructors and discussion leaders to help initiate discussion of the issues the cases raise.

We hope you will find them as interesting, challenging, and useful as we have. We welcome your reactions to individual cases or the collection as a whole.

Norwalk, Connecticut
September 1991

Timothy S. Lucas
Director of Research
and Technical Activities

PREFACE

The cases in this collection cover a variety of important conceptual issues in accounting and are intended to be both interesting and thought provoking. Each case concerns a specific situation, thereby providing an effective vehicle for encapsulating and conveying the essence of complex abstract issues. The brief, one or two-page format of the cases makes them readily digestible and easily remembered.

The cases are presented in alphabetical order by title instead of being organized by issues covered for two reasons. One is to allow the reader to discover the issue(s) contained in the case rather than being told what it (they) might be. The other is that many of the cases contain several issues, rendering categorization difficult if not impossible.

Focus

The cases focus on issues of recognition and measurement in financial statements. In that context, the term *financial statements* refers to what is often called the "body" of the statements, not the accompanying notes. Thus, *disclosure*—reporting outside the body of the statements—is not a focus of the cases.

Booking or *recording* are common shorthand terms for recognition and measurement. More precisely, *recognition* is the process of formally recording or incorporating an item into the financial statements of an entity as an asset, liability, revenue, expense, gain, loss, distribution to owners, or investment by owners. Recognition includes depiction of an item in both words and numbers, with the amount included in the totals of the financial statements. Thus, recognition presupposes simultaneous *measurement,* the quantification of those items in monetary terms so that they can be added to or subtracted from each other.

Potential Audiences

The cases may be used in either formal programs of study or informal study. College and university students may find these cases a useful supplement to their financial accounting textbooks and other course materials. The cases would be particularly useful in courses in intermediate accounting and accounting theory. In that regard, the book is intended to help fill a void that exists in course materials today.

In addition to degree-seeking students in colleges and universities, participants in continuing education programs, both formal and informal, may find this casebook helpful. As life-long learning becomes an increasingly important part of their professional lives, preparers, auditors, and users of financial statements may find this book can help them to develop a deeper understanding of the conceptual underpinnings on which financial statements rest and to understand better today's accounting issues and controversies. Finally, individuals interested in learning more about conceptual issues in accounting may find the cases to be a helpful tool for independent study.

Potential Uses

These cases were originally developed to facilitate the consideration of particular concepts in formulating the FASB's conceptual framework. That conceptual orientation remains a primary purpose of the cases today. Thus, this book may be seen as a springboard to help this generation of students and professionals better understand the real underlying significance of accounting concepts and how they affect accounting practice.

Accordingly, the cases lend themselves particularly well to serving as a basis for critiquing present practice, thereby generating discussion about "what ought to be" as compared with "what is." What are the underlying economics of the transactions or other events in each of the case situations? What is the effect of those "real world" events on the entity or entities involved? How should those effects be reflected in the financial statements? Does present practice reflect those effects adequately or appropriately? Why or why not?

In that regard, "role-playing" may be a useful and interesting means for discussing the cases. By acting in the roles of Board members who are considering those issues at a Board meeting or preparers and auditors who are discussing the contents of financial statements prior to their release, participants could gain meaningful experience in applying the conceptual framework by using it as the basis for their discussion.

Although the primary purpose of the cases is to facilitate conceptual discussions, they can be adapted to other uses as well. The cases can be used as vehicles for researching the current authoritative literature as part of college or professional development courses that concern "accounting research" in a manner akin to how law schools teach "legal research." The cases also can illustrate present practice, demonstrating both applications and limitations of current generally accepted accounting principles.

Regardless of the context in which they are used, the cases can play an important role in developing reasoning skills. "Reasoning by analogy" is an important analytical skill that accounting students must develop and accounting professionals must hone. The cases can be used to analogize to a variety of accounting and reporting situations, including analysis of the pronouncements and current agenda items of the FASB, the Securities and Exchange Commission, the Accounting Standards Executive Committee of the American Institute of Certified Public Accountants, and the FASB's Emerging Issues Task Force, as well as the pronouncements of the FASB's predecessors, the Accounting Principles Board and the Committee on Accounting Procedure of the AICPA.

A Few Words about Concepts

Because this book is about case situations involving accounting concepts, it is appropriate to give some consideration to concepts and their importance. What effect can concepts be expected to have on financial accounting in general and accounting standards in particular? What questions do concepts help answer? With what questions do they not help much? Concepts can be useful to future generations of accounting professionals only if their strengths and limitations are known and understood.

Concepts are an integral part of virtually every body of human knowledge that is called a discipline. The practice of engineering, for example, is based on concepts of mathematics and science. Major construction projects such as bridges and skyscrapers require civil engineering, a discipline that is founded in part on concepts of geometry and physics. The petrochemical industry relies on chemical engineering, a discipline that is deeply rooted in the concepts of chemistry.

The discipline of financial accounting too is based on a foundation of concepts—in this case, concepts rooted in economic activity. On that foundation is built what is referred to as generally accepted accounting principles, the collection of rules, practices, and procedures that guide the form and content of financial statements in the United States.

The conceptual foundation of financial accounting is rooted in observations about the environment in which financial statements are provided and used: the kinds of information financial statements can and cannot provide, the purposes for which those who use financial statements want the information, characteristics of financial statement information that make it useful for those purposes, characteristics of the business entities that the users of the information are interested in, how those characteristics are reflected in the financial statements, and so on. Financial accounting shares with civil and chemical engineering the feature of a conceptual foundation. However, the subject matter of financial accounting is not geometry, physics, chemistry, and the like, but assets and liabilities of business and other entities and the transactions and other events that change assets and liabilities as the entities carry out their functions in the U.S. economy.

The FASB concepts Statements that formulate the conceptual framework for accounting and reporting in the United States are as follows: *Objectives of Fi-*

nancial Reporting by Business Enterprises (No. 1), *Objectives of Financial Reporting by Nonbusiness Organizations* (No. 4), *Qualitative Characteristics of Accounting Information* (No. 2), *Elements of Financial Statements* (No. 6), and *Recognition and Measurement in Financial Statements of Business Enterprises* (No. 5). Those Statements should provide a useful basis for considering many of the issues the cases raise.*

For many other issues, however, the concepts Statements may not be particularly helpful. In some of those instances, the underlying conceptual issues were considered but not resolved by the FASB during the course of its conceptual framework project. In others, the issues may not have been addressed—perhaps because they may have been lower-order issues whose resolution depended on resolution of higher-order issues on which agreement could not be obtained. Whatever the reason, those issues represent especially fertile ground for discussion.

Those discussions should suggest the potential applicability of multiple concepts; some will be competing—inherently contradictory concepts that cannot be applied simultaneously—and others will be complementary. To resolve the cases, therefore, choices will have to be made between competing concepts. Moreover, because certain concepts may follow logically from others, choosing one may necessarily lead to the application of others.

The exercise of making those choices should be revealing. Each of us probably has our own conceptual framework that we use when thinking about financial accounting issues. Those frameworks may have been developed by careful reasoning, or they may simply be more or less intuitive in nature. Some may be more fully thought out than others, and some may be more firmly held than others.

Whatever the basis for one's personal framework, the cases provide a sort of proving ground for it. Discussion of the issues raised in the cases will reveal differences in views, perhaps not unlike the differences in views that arise when Board members discuss FASB agenda items. In the course of those discussions, the strengths and weaknesses of individual concepts should emerge. Participants in those discussions will be challenged to defend their favored views and may find that some of their defenses are not as strong as they might have thought.

The outcomes of those discussions may not lead to complete agreement on each of the issues and the concepts that should be applied in those situations

---

*The concepts Statements are currently offered in a number of publications: (1) *Statements of Financial Accounting Concepts,* available as a separate volume from Richard D. Irwin, Inc., (2) included in Volume II of *Original Pronouncements,* available from the AICPA for its members and from Richard D. Irwin, Inc. for all others, and (3) individual concepts Statements ordered from the FASB.

(however, if the discussion is designed to emulate how the Board might discuss those issues, the outcomes should be based on applicable parts of the FASB's conceptual framework). Nonetheless, the discussions should lead to a better understanding of conceptual differences, why they exist, and what their effects are. If they do, the cases will have served their purpose by contributing to the intellectual growth of aspiring and practicing professionals.

Norwalk, Connecticut
September 1991

L. Todd Johnson
Research Manager

ACKNOWLEDGMENTS

The cases in this collection were written by past and present members of the FASB's Research and Technical Activities (RTA) staff, all of whom were staff members when they wrote the cases. Ascribing the origin or authorship of particular cases to individual staff members is difficult, if not impossible, because development of the cases was very much a team effort, with different individuals contributing at various stages.

Robert R. Sterling, senior fellow (now with the University of Utah), proposed the effort to develop the cases in conjunction with the recognition and measurement phase of the conceptual framework project. Most of the original cases were prepared by a three-person project team: L. Todd Johnson, research manager; Paul B. W. Miller, faculty fellow (now with the University of Colorado at Colorado Springs); and Robert Sterling. Additional cases were prepared by Jeffrey D. Cropsey, practice fellow (now with Phoenix Re Corp.) and Michael J. Fogg, project manager (now with Tellabs International, Inc.). Significant assistance in the preparation of those original cases was also provided by Robert Hampton III (previously with Price Waterhouse, now retired); Diana W. Willis, project manager; and Reed K. Storey, senior technical advisor.

The proposal to supplement the original cases and publish them for use by others originated with James J. Leisenring, Board member, during his tenure as director, RTA. Additional cases to fill certain gaps in the original case set were written by Todd Johnson, who edited all the cases and prepared them for publication, with the assistance of Carol M. Clarke, assistant project manager. Significant assistance in that effort was also provided by Halsey G. Bullen, project manager; James Leisenring; Timothy S. Lucas, director, RTA; David Mosso, assistant director, RTA; and Reed Storey. This book was prepared for publication by the members of the FAF Production Department.

The FASB Cases on Recognition and Measurement

CONTENTS

Page

THE ASSET DISPOSAL CASE

"The sporting thing"

Early in the year, Sweetspot, Inc., a leading manufacturer of quality recreational equipment, put some idle cash to work by investing in marketable securities, some of which later advanced in price while others declined. The securities were recorded at cost.

In November, Martina Nicklaus, president of Sweetspot, decided to dispose of all the securities. The securities were actively traded on the Big Board, with Sweetspot's holdings only a minor fraction of the normal daily volume. As of November 10, the pertinent figures were:

	Cost	Market
Appreciated securities	$40,000	$70,000
Depreciated securities	40,000	27,000
Total	$80,000	$97,000

Because Sweetspot prepares financial statements only at year-end, no gains or losses have been recognized for any of the securities.

President Nicklaus is considering five possible means for disposing of the marketable securities:

1. Sell for cash
2. Use to satisfy liabilities
3. Distribute to stockholders as a dividend
4. Use to pay executive bonuses
5. Donate to charity.

She has told the controller that her decision about which course of action to take will depend in part on how much income or loss will be recognized as a result of the disposal option she chooses.

* * * *

How much income or loss should Sweetspot recognize under each of the five options for disposing of the assets? Should the amount depend on the means of disposal?

1

THE BALTIMORE CANYON CASE

"Taking a plunge"

On December 8, 1981, the Interior Department's Bureau of Land Management (BLM) conducted a sale of offshore oil and gas leases off the mid-Atlantic coast. An ancient subterranean reef passes through the area, creating what is known as the Baltimore Canyon Trough about 100 miles offshore. According to the BLM, "the intermingling of the carbonate reef with the black shales present in the North Atlantic basin would appear to present an ideal situation for the formation of structural petroleum-bearing traps."

The *New York Times* characterized the water depths of up to 8,000 feet as being "well beyond today's technological capacity for offshore production." A consortium of oil companies dominated the bidding, making offers primarily on tracts with depths ranging from 5,000 to 7,000 feet.

On December 23, 1981, the Interior Department accepted high bids of nearly $322 million for 50 of the tracts. The highest single bid was for $41 million that the consortium offered for Wilmington Canyon Block 587. That bid was almost $33 million higher than the second highest bid for that tract.

In its 1981 annual report, one of the members of the consortium stated:

> In December, we were very successful in a major lease sale in the mid-Atlantic by acquiring, with others, 26 tracts for a bonus cost of $266 million ([our] share $157 million). We believe these tracts largely overlie a buried reef complex. Water depths are up to 7,000 feet—a truly deepwater frontier area. While the costs and economic risks of operations in these water depths are high, if successful, this setting could be the source of prolific oil or gas production.

*   *   *   *

Should the members of the consortium recognize the lease for Block 587 as an asset when acquired and, if so, at what amount?

2

THE BANK LOAN CASE

"So, what do I owe?"

Business at Juan Braun's Body Shop is brisk. The shop is filled with automobiles damaged in "fender-bender" accidents on streets and highways glazed in a recent ice storm. Many of the cars to be repaired are expensive imports for which Braun must order parts from abroad. Although the owners of those cars are insured, Braun cannot collect for parts and labor until the repairs are complete and claims checks are released by the insurance carriers. Because Braun must prepay for the parts orders, he must take out a short-term loan to provide the needed working capital to repair the cars.

Braun obtained a $60,000 bank loan on October 1 in the name of his business. The face interest rate is 13 percent per annum, and both interest and principal are due in a single payment 12 months hence.

The loan contract contains several important provisions. One is that the loan is not assumable by any other party: should Braun die, sell his business, or otherwise lose control of it, both principal and interest accrued to date become payable on demand. Another entitles Braun to pay off the loan at any time simply by repaying the principal and interest accrued to date: the contract states that the bank earns interest based on the "rule of 78s method."

Early in December, Braun learned that he would be receiving an unexpectedly large inheritance from his uncle. The executor of the estate notified him that his bequest of nearly $80,000 would be paid in cash on January 1. Having no other pressing needs for the funds, Braun is contemplating investing them in his business to wipe out the bank loan.

The body shop's books are maintained on a calendar-year basis. Interest rates for notes of similar terms and quality as Braun's have remained unchanged through the end of the current year.

*   *   *   *

a. How should Juan Braun's Body Shop report the loan on its year-end financial statements? Should his intent to repay or not repay the loan early affect the accounting?

b. Assume Braun had to pay one point as a nonrefundable "loan inception fee," which Mark Deutsche, the loan officer, explained as "necessary to cover the costs of the credit check and other paperwork relative to the loan." How should the fee be reported on the year-end statements?

THE BARTER CASE

"Will that be cash?"

Ben Sawyer had started handcrafting replicas of antique furniture as a retirement hobby, but at the urging of friends he later opened a small shop to sell his products. It proved an immediate success, first with the "summer people" and then with dealers, several of whom encouraged Ben to supplement his line of small tables and bookcases with larger pieces. Ben decided to give it a try. After closing the shop for the winter, he worked in the basement of his home designing an impressive mahogany sideboard and building two of them by the shop's spring reopening. Materials costs (for wood) amounted to $600 for each; Ben's labor, priced at the going wage rate was $400 for each. No overhead costs were incurred.

Although familiar with the market of casual "antique" furnishings, Ben was uncertain about an appropriate price for his sideboards. From a review of catalogues offering pieces mass-produced from cheaper woods, he concluded that a figure of $2,000 to $3,000 was about right for handcrafted mahogany. Accordingly, he priced each sideboard at $2,500 ("and I'm ready to haggle if somebody's ready to buy," he told Mrs. Sawyer).

Within one week, Ben sold both sideboards with no haggling. He sold the first one on reopening day to Will Bascomb, a dealer he knew well. "Beautiful work, Ben," said Will. "I want it, but I'm going to be short of cash for a while. How about $500 down and the balance in quarterly installments for a year?" Done. Cash, a non-interest-bearing note, and sideboard changed hands.

The second sale came two days later. Seth Forester, Ben's wood supplier since the hobby-only days, dropped by to see if Ben needed any materials and was captivated by the sideboard. "I don't remember when I last had $2,500 in one lump," said Seth, "and I don't reckon to have it anytime soon. But craftsmen like you always need wood. How about if I pay you in wood—enough for mine and three others. Wood for sideboard, OK?" OK.

When Mrs. Sawyer returned from a week in Florida, Ben hastened to tell her the good news that both sideboards had sold. "That's great, Ben!" she said. "How much did we get for them?"

*   *   *   *

a. How should Sawyer recognize the sideboard sales?
b. How should Will and Seth recognize the sideboard purchases?

4

THE BOND CASE

"'Tis not in the bond . . ."

On December 31, 1979, registration of Winton Company's 10-year, 16 percent debentures, interest payable annually, became effective, and the entire issue of $10,000,000 was sold at par. Trading on the New York Stock Exchange began at once and continued for the life of the issue, in sufficient daily volume to result in reliable quotations.

Market prices for "Winton 16s" varied widely during the period, reflecting the trend of interest rates. At the end of each of the 10 years in point, the closing prices and the related market interest rates to maturity were as follows:

December 31	Price	Yield
1980	95.5	17%
1981	88.1	19
1982	104.2	15
1983	116.4	12
1984	122.8	10
1985	115.5	11
1986	97.8	17
1987	98.4	17
1988	97.4	19
1989	100.0	—

Among the investors in Winton 16s were two corporations, Alewife Enterprises and Beadle Holdings, Ltd. Each bought $1,000,000 face amount at market— Alewife on December 31, 1981 and Beadle two years later—and held the bonds to maturity.

Winton, Alewife, and Beadle all face the same accounting question: measurement of the debentures and of related amounts recognized in income. Under existing practice, "the answer" is as follows (dollars in thousands):

12/31	WINTON		ALEWIFE		BEADLE	
	Liability	Expense	Asset	Income	Asset	Income
1979	$10,000	$ —	$ —	$ —	$ —	$ —
1980	10,000	1,600	—	—	—	—
1981	10,000	1,600	881	—	—	—
1982	10,000	1,600	889	168	—	—
1983	10,000	1,600	898	169	1,164	—
1984	10,000	1,600	908	170	1,144	140
1985	10,000	1,600	921	173	1,122	138
1986	10,000	1,600	936	175	1,096	132
1987	10,000	1,600	954	178	1,068	132
1988	10,000	1,600	975	181	1,036	128
1989	10,000/0	1,600	1,000/0	185	1,000/0	124
		$16,000		$1,399		$796

Nevertheless, uneasiness about "the answer" persists in the minds of Winton's controller, Alewife's treasurer, and Beadle's finance director, who have worked up some different numbers, based on market, as follows (dollars in thousands):

12/31	WINTON		ALEWIFE		BEADLE	
	Liability	Expense	Asset	Income	Asset	Income
1979	$10,000	$ —	$ —	$ —	$ —	$ —
1980	9,550	1,150	—	—	—	—
1981	8,810	860	881	—	—	—
1982	10,420	3,210	1,042	321	—	—
1983	11,640	2,820	1,164	282	1,164	—
1984	12,280	2,240	1,228	224	1,228	224
1985	11,550	870	1,155	87	1,155	87
1986	9,780	(170)	978	(17)	978	(17)
1987	9,840	1,660	984	166	984	166
1988	9,740	1,500	974	150	974	150
1989	10,000/0	1,860	1,000/0	186	1,000/0	186
		$16,000		$1,399		$796

*　*　*　*

a. What are the pros and cons of each set of figures?
b. If, after 1982, the bond prices reflected higher ratings for the issue by Moody's and Standard & Poor's, how—if at all—should that affect the accounting for the bonds?

THE BONUS CASE

"Cashing in"

Audie Torr, an aspiring young CPA, has just joined the staff of Foote & Tick, a local public accounting firm. Located in a rapidly expanding suburban area, the firm has enjoyed double-digit annual growth in both clients and revenues.

Because of the area's growth, many opportunities are available to young professionals. The field is rich for "hanging out your own shingle," and many existing firms are staff poor. As a consequence, Foote & Tick has suffered heavy staff turnover almost since its inception 10 years ago. The typical staff member has left after only two or three years either to join a larger firm or to establish a practice on his or her own. Turnover is so high that clients are complaining about the lack of continuity in the staff servicing their own accounts.

In order to entice staff members to stay with the firm, Foote & Tick has decided to implement a new "longevity bonus" program. Its terms provide for a one-time cash bonus to be paid to each employee upon the completion of five years of continuous employment. The amount of each bonus will be the sum of 10 percent of the salary paid in each of the 5 years of employment. With the bonus, the partners anticipate that about half of the new hires will still be employed after five years.

Audie Torr is the first employee to be hired under the new bonus plan. His first year's salary is to be $25,000. The partners expect that his salary will be about $35,000 in the 5th year and will average about $30,000 over the 5-year period.

* * * *

How should the firm recognize the bonus to Audie Torr?

THE CHEMICAL PLANT CASE

"Waste not . . ."

Chemico owns and operates petrochemical plants on the Gulf coasts of Louisiana and Texas. To meet the booming demand for its products, Chemico is building a new, state-of-the-art petrochemical plant at Rougetown that will complement its existing facilities there. Although Chemico will have plenty of productive capacity in about 3 years when the new plant is fully operational, maintaining its 32 percent share of the booming market in the meantime may be difficult.

To fill its interim needs, Chemico entered into negotiations with the trustee for Oxxyn, a bankrupt corporation undergoing liquidation. The trustee already had disposed of all Oxxyn's facilities except for one, the Muddy Bayou Plant. A state-of-the-art plant when it was built some 25 years ago, Muddy Bayou is becoming obsolete and will not be economically viable much longer. However, as Muddy Bayou has sufficient productive capacity to satisfy its short-term needs, Chemico purchased the plant for a cash price of $10 million.

Chemico plans to operate Muddy Bayou until Rougetown is ready, after which it plans to dismantle the plant and sell the site. Plant dismantlement costs are expected to be $2 million, net of recoveries from salvaged materials and equipment.

In addition, new environmental regulations mandate the cleanup of the plant site's soil of all hazardous substances; failure to do so will result in onerous fines and penalties. Aware of the new regulations before entering into negotiations with Oxxyn's trustee, Chemico had factored the cost of cleanup into the purchase price. Following the cleanup, expected to cost $1 million, the sales value of the land will be about $5 million.

* * * *

a. How should Chemico recognize the cleanup cost? Would the answer be different if Chemico either had not been aware of the new regulations or had not factored the expected cost of cleanup into the purchase price?
b. Assume instead the cleanup is expected to cost $4 million. How should it be recognized?

THE CORN AND HOGS CASE (PART I)

"Growing corn"

A third-generation farmer, Frank Seedman was delighted to have been able to acquire Fertile Acres Farm for its many attractive features. Soil and topography were ideal for growing corn, with additional land and ample water for raising livestock as well. The farm also offered ready access to a year-round local grain and livestock market, sufficiently active to assure day-to-day prices approximating those prevailing in major agricultural centers. Moreover, because of the market's proximity, transportation costs were negligible.

The farm was inactive when Seedman bought it, the previous owner having retired in the winter and moved to Florida. Corn-growing had been the previous owner's only activity; the crop was planted in early spring, harvested in early fall, and sold immediately at post-harvest prices. Seedman, however, envisaged a larger operation with more flexibility. He planned to grow more corn and add a hog feedlot, and depending on market conditions, he would decide each year on one of three strategies: (1) sell all the corn at market, (2) sell some of the corn and use the rest for hog feed, or (3) use all of the corn for feed. Adopting either the second or third strategy would maintain flexibility since Seedman could readily sell some or all the hogs, buy more hogs, sell the corn held for feed, or buy more corn for feed.

Seedman decided not to buy any hogs until his first corn crop was harvested so that he would have the option of being able to use it for feed. He spent $10,000 for seed, fertilizer, and so forth, to grow 10,000 bushels of corn. Planting was completed in early May and the whole crop was harvested at the end of September. The prevailing market price for corn was $2.90 per bushel on June 30 and $3.00 on September 30, when he sold half the crop.

* * * *

a. Should Seedman recognize any profit on the corn on his June 30 quarterly financial statements? If so, how much?
b. What amount of profit on the corn should Seedman recognize on his September 30 quarterly financial statements? Are there any features about the farming business that should differentiate it from other kinds of business for accounting purposes?

9

THE CORN AND HOGS CASE (PART II)

"Raising hogs"

Immediately after harvesting the corn, Seedman bought 100 feeder pigs for $150 each, using the proceeds from selling the 5,000 bushels of corn.

The only cost of raising the pigs was feed, and Seedman decided to feed his pigs exclusively from the corn he harvested. By December 31, he had fed 900 bushels of corn to the pigs and sold an equal amount at the average market price during the period of $3.30 per bushel. By year-end, the market price of corn had risen to $3.40, and the market price of the partially matured hogs was $350 each.

At the end of February, Seedman sold all of his hogs—now fully matured—for $500 each. In January and February, he fed them another 800 bushels of corn and sold another 800 at the average market price during the period of $3.60 per bushel. On the date he sold the hogs, the market price of corn was $3.65 per bushel. At the end of March, Seedman sold the remaining corn for $3.70 per bushel.

*   *   *   *

a. Should Seedman recognize any profit on hogs on his December 31 quarterly financial statements? How much should he recognize on corn?
b. What profit should Seedman recognize on corn and hogs on his March 31 year-end financial statements?

THE FOREIGN CASH CASE (PART I)

"It's a lot of moola . . ."

Americo is an import-export company domiciled in the United States. On the last day of its fiscal year, Americo entered into a transaction with Overseas Supply Company, located in Chaipan, a Pacific Rim country, to purchase 2,000 video cassette recorders (VCRs). The transaction was denominated in the foreign currency unit of Chaipan, the moola (M). The price established was M500 per VCR, for a total price of M1,000,000. The transaction will be completed in another day or two, and because Americo only had M700,000 on hand, it obtained the remaining M300,000 needed through the foreign exchange office of its local bank.

The M700,000 Americo had on hand were the result of two recent events. On December 15, Americo entered into a transaction with another Chaipan company, Orient Traders, for the sale by Americo of 5,000 tons of grain for M100 per ton. The transaction was fully consummated on that date, with title to the grain (in a grain elevator at the port) passing to Orient Traders in exchange for the M500,000, which was delivered to Americo.

The other M200,000 on hand was the result of an aborted transaction in which Americo was to have purchased portable radios from another company in Chaipan. Americo had acquired the moola through the foreign exchange office of its local bank on December 1 in anticipation of completing the deal that day. However, when the radios turned out to be of substandard quality, Americo rejected them and cancelled the deal.

Americo's controller's department determined the spot rates for moola were as follows:

December 1	December 15	December 31
M1 = $0.64	M1 = $0.57	M1 = $0.60

* * * *

How should Americo report the M1,000,000 on its year-end balance sheet?

THE FOREIGN CASH CASE (PART II)

"Buying or selling?"

Americo's controller walked into his office on Monday morning to find his phone ringing. "That you, Elwood?" the caller asked. Immediately recognizing the gravelly voice as that of Bertrand Bigbucks, Americo's CEO, Elwood replied, somewhat anxiously, "Sure is, Chief! What can I do for you this fine day?"

"I was looking at those numbers that your department prepared regarding the translation of that moola we're holding into dollars. Near as I can tell, your staff seems to think there's only one spot rate, but I know there are two quoted—the rate the banks buy foreign cash at and the one they sell it at. Which one did they use here?"

"Neither one, Chief," Elwood responded. "Rather than complicate matters, they averaged the two rates on each date and used that."

"Tarnation!" Bigbucks thundered. "You number crunchers have a fixation about averaging. 'Most everything coming out of your department is averaged. So you're telling me that the numbers I see here are not based on the real rates at all—am I right?"

Elwood swallowed hard. "Well, yes, Chief, I guess so . . ."

"I want those translations to be based on the real spot rates and I want them now," Bigbucks interrupted. "Those averages don't correspond to anything."

"Sure thing, Chief. Have them to you in a few minutes," Elwood replied. Checking his work papers, Elwood found the data the averages were based on, which were as follows:

	December 1	December 15	December 31
Buying rate	M1 = $0.63	M1 = $0.56	M1 = $0.59
Selling price	M1 = $0.65	M1 = $0.58	M1 = $0.61

Scratching his head, Elwood remembered the reason that he and his staff decided to use averages was that they couldn't agree on which rate to use on each date.

* * * *

How should Americo translate the M1,000,000 on its year-end balance sheet?

THE FREQUENT FLIER CASE

"A pretty fair fare . . ."

Late in November, Acme Airlines, a new regional carrier, inaugurated its own frequent flier program to compete more effectively with established carriers. To differentiate its program from those of its competitors, Acme adopted a plan based on the number of flights rather than miles flown. Named the "Fly-Five-Then-Free" program, it offers a free, unrestricted round-trip ticket for every five paid round-trip flights taken.

With load factors ranging between 60 and 65 percent, Acme has sufficient excess capacity to accommodate the free rides. Seats are generally available even on popular flights because of no-shows since most business travelers use Acme's full-fare tickets, which impose no penalty for missing the flight. Thus, management thinks fare-paying passengers will rarely if ever have to be turned away to accommodate the free rides. Acme therefore projects program costs to consist mainly of additional on-board meals (about $3 each) and ticket-writing (about $2 each).

The program also is designed to entice local companies to have their employees fly Acme on business trips. Under its "Corporate Partners" program, Acme credits member companies (rather than the traveler) for a free round-trip for every 5 business round-trips taken.

Hometown, Inc. immediately signed up for Acme's Corporate Partners plan and directed that Acme be used for all business trips to cities it serves. Willard Finster, the company's controller, anticipates each free trip earned will save Hometown about $300. By year-end, Hometown has accrued 10 free trips.

Both Acme and Hometown maintain their accounting records on a calendar-year basis.

* * * *

a. How should Hometown report the 10 free trips it is carrying over to the next calendar year?
b. How should Acme report the 10 free trips that Hometown has earned?

THE GASOLINE TANK CASE

"Taking gas"

Andre Preneur has been looking for a well-located site for a new *haute cuisine* restaurant he plans to open. After an extensive search, he identified an ideal location at the intersection of two well-traveled roads. Following some hard negotiating, Preneur bought the property for $600,000.

On the site was a vacant gasoline station, which had last been rented out to an automobile mechanic who operated it as a muffler shop. That tenant used only the service bays and the office space; no gasoline was sold nor were the underground gasoline tanks used.

Preneur bought the property with the intent of demolishing the gasoline station building (which did not suit his needs for the restaurant) and constructing a new building on the site. Bids he obtained for the demolition ranged from a low of $15,000 to a high of $25,000. Cost of the new building is expected to be between $700,000 and $800,000.

In the process of obtaining the necessary permits for demolition, Preneur learned of a new governmental regulation that requires abandoned underground gasoline tanks to be removed and disposed of when former gasoline stations are demolished. In addition, the regulation requires that any soil contamination that might have eventuated from a leaking tank be treated by refining the soil.

The lowest cost estimate Preneur was able to obtain for removing and disposing of the 3 underground tanks totals $50,000; should refinement of the soil also be necessary, that will cost an additional $40,000.

* * * *

a. How should Andre Preneur recognize the costs of demolishing the gas station, removing the abandoned underground tanks, and refining the soil?
b. Assuming he had been aware of the regulation when purchasing the property, how should he recognize the costs?

THE GENERAL CONTRACTOR CASE

"Home, sweet home!"

Bilderco is a general contractor that constructs and sells single-family homes. Some of its homes are built entirely by its own crews, but others involve using subcontractors. When the market is strong and its sales force sells more homes than its own crews can build, Bilderco farms out the overload.

Even on jobs that are 100 percent subcontracted, Bilderco can turn a profit because of its experience in building from a limited set of stock plans. Having a good feel for the costs of all phases of construction enables Bilderco to drive hard bargains with its subcontractors. The subcontractors are a skilled and dependable lot who are anxious to please a big volume operator like Bilderco. All are fully bonded and will absorb any late penalties Bilderco must pay as a result of their failures.

Sharp is being transferred to the area in six months and has contracted to buy one of Bilderco's "Country Squire" homes. To protect himself from a forthcoming price increase, Sharp has agreed to pay the entire $125,000 price in advance (including $25,000 for the lot). The terms of the contract call for Sharp's new house to be ready for occupancy no later than 6 months from the date of signing, with a $1,000 per week penalty for each week thereafter that the house is not ready.

Bilderco has firm prices from subcontractors for each of the three major phases of construction, as well as good estimates of what it would cost to have its own crews do the job, as follows:

Job Phase	Subcontractors	Bilderco Crews
Foundation	$18,000	$12,000
Structural	45,000	36,000
Systems (plumbing, electrical, etc.)	25,000	24,000
	$88,000	$72,000

The job was completed on schedule, with Bilderco's crews doing only the foundation work, which totalled $12,200.

* * * *

a. When should Bilderco recognize profit on the sale and construction of the house?
b. If Bilderco completed the job six weeks late (four of which were due to subcontractors), how should it recognize the penalty?

THE HEALTH SPA CASE

"Let's get physical!"

Hardy Hearts is a health spa located in a rapidly growing suburban area populated largely by young professionals. Like other spas, memberships are its lifeblood. Typical of its contracts is the one it sold on January 1 to Felicia Footer, a young CPA. She agreed to an $850 contract for a 2-year initial membership, paid the usual $45 down payment, and signed a note for 23 monthly installments of $35 each. Hardy Hearts then sold the note without recourse to a local bank for $640.

As part of the initial membership agreement, Hardy Hearts provides new members with an evaluation of their physical conditioning needs and tailors personalized programs to suit those needs. The spa then periodically assesses each member's program, charts progress to date, and suggests adjustments and modifications as appropriate. However, the employees of Hardy Hearts have little if any specific training in physical fitness.

Member interest in Hardy Hearts wanes quickly. About three-fourths of new members use the spa's facilities regularly for only the first three months; afterwards, their usage is sporadic or nonexistent, with few renewing their memberships. As a result, Hardy Hearts sells many more memberships at lower prices than otherwise would be possible by "overselling" the spa's physical capacity.

Hardy Hearts spends 40 percent of its membership revenue on sales commissions and other direct selling efforts and maintains its facilities in "showroom" condition (the added cost for which is not readily determinable). Other expenses are largely fixed (rent, depreciation, utilities, and so forth) and involve making the facility available for use by its members. Those costs average $10 per month per contract, or $240 over a 2-year membership.

The membership contracts contain a clause permitting Hardy Hearts to assign its obligations to its members to any subsequent owner of the facility. Although changes in ownership are not frequent, the industry's "rule of thumb" is for the buyer of the facility to charge the seller about $12 per month per membership for any remaining obligations for which the buyer assumes responsibility.

* * * *

How should Hardy Hearts recognize income from Footer's membership in each of the two years?

16

THE HULA HOOP CASE

"Let's twist again"

I. M. Sanguine, the sole proprietor of the Chula Vista Toy Company, is bullish on hula hoops. Even though the fad faded away many years ago, Sanguine is convinced that it will return by next Christmas. Other toy manufacturers disagree, and none have any inventories of hula hoops nor do they plan to manufacture any. Although they view Sanguine as an oddball who marches to a different drummer, they do acknowledge that on a few occasions his off-the-wall forecasts have proven correct. More often, however, they just have been off the wall.

Acting on what he described as his gut feeling, Sanguine bought raw materials (primarily plastic) for $1,000 cash and pulled an old, fully depreciated (and valueless) extruder out of storage. Operating the extruder himself in the evenings after his workers had gone for the day, he produced 2,000 units of finished product, which he planned to store until Christmas when they would be marketed under the trademark "Chula Hoops." Because the proprietor furnished all the labor and there was no depreciation or overhead, the finished goods were accounted for as follows:

Raw materials inventory	1,000	
Cash		1,000

To record purchase of raw materials

Work-in-process inventory	1,000	
Raw materials inventory		1,000

To record putting the raw materials into process

Finished goods inventory	1,000	
Work-in-process inventory		1,000

To record the completion of the production process

*   *   *   *

Should the "Chula Hoops" be recognized as assets and, if so, at what amount?

THE INSTANT MILLIONAIRE CASE

"And the winner is . . . Shirley Lucky!"

Shirley Lucky has just won the Instant Millionaire Prize in the Magazine Clearinghouse Sweepstakes. The prize is payable in installments of $50,000 on January 1 for each of the next 20 years.

Because it pays in installments rather than in a lump sum, Magazine Clearinghouse has been criticized by various consumer groups for what they regard as false advertising in how the prize is labeled. Given continued inflation, they argue that the winner never does become a millionaire in fact because the dollars paid in future years are worth less in purchasing power than those when the winner is announced.

Stung by the criticism, Magazine Clearinghouse has decided to modify the award to Shirley Lucky. Although it would prefer to mute the criticism by paying the award all at once, it cannot do so because of a cash crunch; hence, another alternative has been adopted. Payments will be made over the 20-year period as before, but each payment will be adjusted for inflation, using the government's general cost-of-living index to adjust each installment to the purchasing power equivalent of what $50,000 would have bought in the year Shirley Lucky won her prize.

The annual rate of inflation has ranged between 3 and 5 percent for the past 5 years, with the rate for the most recent year being 3.9 percent. However, in the preceding 5-year period, inflation rates ranged between 6 percent and 17 percent, with the average being 11.2 percent. Inflation rates in the preceding decade averaged 5 percent. Economists are loathe to predict future long-term inflation rates, but they do generally expect next year's prices to increase at a rate on par with this year's. Interest rates tend to approximate the inflation rate plus 4 points (for example, with 5 percent inflation, the interest rate would be about 9 percent).

* * * *

What liability should Magazine Clearinghouse recognize? Should an indexed promise be accounted for the same as an unindexed promise?

THE INSURANCE CASE

"We've got you covered"

Inscorp is a property and liability insurance company that both writes policies and underwrites various kinds of casualty risks. Inscorp carries many of the policies that it writes, but also transfers some to other carriers so that its exposure in any geographical area or risk class does not become excessive.

The only insurance companies that Inscorp deals with have proven themselves to be both reliable and financially sound. Many of the risks Inscorp insures are transferred to Reinco, a major reinsurance carrier, because of its fine reputation for handling policyholder claims quickly and fairly. In the many years it has been in the business, Reinco has never defaulted on a policy transferred to it from Inscorp or any other company.

Inscorp has written two fire insurance policies, one for Hill and the other for Dale. The policies are virtually identical, both being for 3-year terms with face amounts of $3,000,000, and the policyholders are in the same risk class. In return for a favorable premium discount ($7,000 on each policy), Hill and Dale both have agreed to the following conditions:

1. The policies are noncancellable by either party.
2. The policies may be transferred without recourse to any one of five listed insurance companies (of which Reinco is one).
3. The entire three-year premium must be paid in advance.

After the $7,000 discount, each policy has a premium of $50,000. Sales commissions are 10 percent of the premium, and policy-writing costs (including direct inspection and policy issue costs) amount to $1,000 per policy. Inscorp expects the claims costs under policies in this group to be 70 percent of the premiums collected.

Reinco will accept either or both of the policies for the standard industry fee of 80 percent of the original policy premium. However, Inscorp decided to transfer only one and keep the other. Because it was indifferent about which to retain, Inscorp arbitrarily kept the Hill policy and transferred the Dale one.

* * * *

What income should Inscorp recognize on the Hill and Dale policies?

THE LIABILITY OR EQUITY CASE (PART I)

"It's a debt! It's an equity! It's, it's . . . !"

Kids & Co., a medium-sized toy manufacturer, issued convertible bonds with a face value of $50 million. Each of the 50,000 bonds was issued at its face value of $1,000. The coupon interest rate, payable semiannually, is 7.8 percent. Except for the interest rate and the conversion feature, all of the terms of the convertible bond are the same as the terms of outstanding issues of otherwise comparable nonconvertible debt. The market interest rate for otherwise comparable nonconvertible debt is 10 percent; in that interest rate environment, similar debt with the same face value could have been issued for approximately $40 million.

The controller, Barb E. Dahl, asked her new staff accountant, Ted E. Baer, to prepare the entries to record the issuance of the convertible bonds. Two days later, she was surprised to discover that Ted was struggling to prepare the entries. When asked what the problem was, Ted responded that he could not decide whether a portion of the $50 million issuance proceeds should be attributed to the conversion feature.

*　　*　　*　　*

Should Kids & Co. account for the convertible bonds as a simple liability, or should it account separately for the components?

THE LIABILITY OR EQUITY CASE (PART II)

"If it looks like a duck . . ."

On January 2, 19X0, Kids & Co. issued 100,000 shares of mandatorily redeemable preferred stock with cumulative dividends at a rate of 8 percent. The stock was issued for $50 per share, and its terms call for Kids & Co. to redeem it on December 31, 19X9 for $50 per share plus accrued but unpaid dividends, whether declared or not. The stock is senior to all other stock of the enterprise; the seniority provisions prohibit declaration or payment of dividends to other stock unless the full cumulative dividend has been declared or set aside for payment. Redemption is not optional on the part of either the issuer or the holder.

Staff accountant Ted E. Baer had a question for the controller, Barb E. Dahl. "Barb," he said, "if Kids & Co. wanted to raise capital for a fixed period at a fixed cost, why did it issue mandatorily redeemable preferred stock instead of straight debt?"

Barb answered, "One of the benefits of our issuing the preferred stock is that we don't have to report the dividends as an expense and deduct them in determining net income, although, like all preferred dividends, we do deduct them to determine income available for common stockholders."

"Something doesn't seem right to me," said Ted. "Mandatorily redeemable preferred stock and straight debt seem similar economically, but if Kids & Co. had issued debt, the payments of interest and at least some changes in the value of the liability would be reported in income, whereas with the preferred stock there is no effect on net income. Moreover, the interest would be deductible for income tax purposes while the preferred dividends aren't."

Barb said, "I see your point. Why don't you do some research and see what you can find about mandatorily redeemable preferred stock."

Ted researched the accounting literature and found the SEC's Accounting Series Release No. 268, *Presentation in Financial Statements of "Redeemable Preferred Stocks"* (as codified in SEC Financial Reporting Release 1, *Codification of Financial Reporting Policies*), which prohibits a public company from displaying with its equity instruments stock that is redeemable other than at the election of the issuer. The effect of that requirement is to treat mandatorily redeemable preferred stock as temporary equity. Ted still does not understand why an obligation with a fixed maturity date and amount, such as mandatorily redeemable preferred stock, is not accounted for as a liability. Barb is having similar doubts.

*   *   *   *

a. How should Kids & Co. record the issuance of mandatorily redeemable preferred stock?
b. Would the answer be different if Kids & Co. were not a public company?

THE LIABILITY OR EQUITY CASE (PART III)

"A pig in a poke"

Kids & Co. offers a generous employee compensation package that includes employee stock options. The exercise price of an option always has been equal to the market price of the stock at the date of grant. Kids & Co.'s controller, Barb E. Dahl, believes that employee stock options, like all obligations of an enterprise to issue its own stock, are equity instruments, not liabilities. Staff accountant Ted E. Baer is responsible for employee compensation issues, and he is not sure that he agrees with Barb's conclusion. He is determined to resolve the issue before lunch.

Ted knocked on the door to Barb's office before she poured her first cup of coffee. "Barb," he said, "I don't understand the accounting for employee stock options. Don't you agree that when a company issues stock for less than its current value, it dilutes the value of the other stockholders' holdings?"

"Well, yes, . . ." Barb began.

Ted interrupted, "I don't understand why that dilution isn't recognized as an expense or loss in measuring the company's net income."

Barb said, "Under the FASB's definition of liabilities, an obligation to issue stock isn't a liability because it doesn't involve an obligation to transfer assets or provide future services. Moreover, from the employee's point of view, a stock option is kind of like a pig in a poke. The employee hopes that he can make some real money out of having the option, but that can't happen unless the stock price appreciates. As for the dilution you mentioned, a distribution to owners that benefits one group of owners at the expense of another doesn't result in a gain or loss to the company itself."

Ted said, "I still don't understand. Why isn't an obligation to issue stock at less than the market price on the date of delivery a liability? If the terms of a future issuance of stock have the potential to be unfavorable to the company's present stockholders, why aren't the terms unfavorable to the company itself? Why don't those terms affect the company's reported financial performance?"

* * * *

How should Kids & Co. account for its employee stock options?

THE LOAN COMMITMENT FEE CASE

"Hatfield and McCoy"

Jim Eger, lending officer of the Hatfield Trust Company, was pleased by the unexpected visit of C. Norbert Gotrocks, chairman of the town's leading industrial company.

Mr. Gotrocks was blunt. "We've always banked with your big rivals over at McCoy National, Jim, but this time they can't hack it. Looks like it's time to rethink our banking arrangements, and I hope you agree.

"If our offer for Mountain Products goes through, we'll need a 3-year, $1,000,000 loan—and we'll need it fast. What I want from Hatfield Trust is a six-month commitment for that loan, at prime on the date we get the money. Can do?"

Jim thought briefly. No problem with the amount: well within the bank's single-borrower limit and a fraction of what Jim would be willing to lend Gotrocks Industries if there were no limit. As to committing a million to short-term loans at the lower overnight funds rate, no real problem there, either—that's what commitment fees are for.

"Can do and delighted to, Mr. Gotrocks," said Jim. "The commitment fee will be $10,000, nonrefundable and payable in cash when we sign, which we can do this afternoon. I'll call you when the papers are ready."

*   *   *   *

a. Hatfield's debit is to Cash, but what should the credit be? When and for how much?
b. Gotrocks Industries' credit is to Cash, but what should the debit be? When and for how much?

THE LOTTERY TICKET CASE (PART I)

"Taking a long shot . . ."

To supplement donations collected from its general community solicitation, Tri-Cities United Charities holds an Annual Lottery Sweepstakes. In this year's sweepstakes, United Charities is offering a grand prize of $1,000,000 to the 1 winning ticket. A total of 10,000 tickets have been printed and United Charities plans to sell all the tickets at a price of $150 each.

Since its inception, the Sweepstakes has attracted area-wide interest, and United Charities has always been able to meet its sales target. However, in the unlikely eventuality that it might fail to sell a sufficient number of tickets to cover the grand prize, United Charities has reserved the right to cancel the Sweepstakes and to refund the price of the tickets to holders.

In recent years, a fairly active secondary market for tickets has developed. This year, buying-selling prices have varied between $75 and $95 before stabilizing at about $90.

When the tickets first went on sale this year, multimillionaire Phil N. Tropic, well-known in Tri-Cities civic circles as a generous but sometimes eccentric donor, bought one of the tickets from United Charities, paying $150 in cash.

* * * *

a. Should Phil N. Tropic recognize his lottery ticket as an asset and, if so, at what amount?
b. Assume that the lottery tickets were nontransferable and no secondary market developed. Should Tropic recognize the lottery ticket as an asset and, if so, at what amount?

THE LOTTERY TICKET CASE (PART II)

"Tilting the odds . . ."

In order to generate increased enthusiasm about the next year's lottery, United Charities decided that the single grand prize of $1,000,000 would be replaced by a number of smaller prizes. The following schedule of prizes was established:

1 "grand" prize of $100,000	(=	$ 100,000)
10 "gold" prizes of $10,000 each	(=	100,000)
100 "silver" prizes of $1,000 each	(=	100,000)
1,000 "bronze" prizes of $300 each	(=	300,000)
4,000 "tin" prizes of $100 each	(=	400,000)
5,111		(= $1,000,000)

The total number of tickets to be issued remained at 10,000 at a price of $150 per ticket.

Because of the increased chances of getting a winning ticket, sales of tickets this year have been exceptionally brisk, with United Charities selling out its entire stock of 10,000 tickets in the first week the tickets were offered for sale. As in previous years, a secondary market for tickets again developed with prices settling at about $110 per ticket.

Once again among the purchasers was Phil N. Tropic who, like last year, purchased a ticket for himself.

* * * *

a. Should Phil N. Tropic recognize his lottery ticket as an asset and, if so, at what amount?
b. Assume that instead of keeping the ticket himself, Tropic gave the ticket to his church. Should the church recognize it as an asset and, if so, at what amount?

26

THE MAGAZINE SUBSCRIPTION CASE (PART I)

"Such a deal I'm going to make you . . ."

"*Handyperson's Weekly* got where it is on single-copy sales to ordinary Joes and Janes with six bits in their pockets," said the publisher, "and the whole idea of subscriptions still bothers me a little. How are we making out with it, Swifty?"

"Just great, J. B.," said the marketing director. "The 20 freebies did it: 104-issues-for-the-price-of-84 wowed 'em—never mind the nonrefund policy. We have in already 4,000 2-year subscriptions for this year and next and we're zeroing in on another hot target group next month. I'm telling you, J. B., it is just fantastic!"

The publisher turned to the controller. "What's it all mean financially, Stick?"

"Based on present per-copy cost and estimated fulfillment expenses, we should clear about $22 per 2-year subscription," the controller said. "Maybe a little more or a little less, but no maybe about that $252,000 in the till. All ours, and a sweet boost for our bankroll . . ."

"And for our current earnings," the publisher broke in. "Right?"

"Absolutely! No question whatsoever, J. B., $88,000 straight to this year's bottom line!" said the marketing director, with the year-end bonus firmly in mind.

"Uh, I think we should discuss it a bit, sir," said the controller, with the year-end audit firmly in mind.

*   *   *   *

What liability (if any) should be recognized for the subscriptions upon their receipt and at the end of the first of the two years?

THE MAGAZINE SUBSCRIPTION CASE (PART II)

"Let's do it again"

"Your idea to offer 104-issues-for-the-price-of-84 again this year was equally successful as last year, Swifty!" the publisher exclaimed, patting the marketing director on the back. "Stick here tells me that the final tallies show 4,000 new 2-year subscriptions at $63 apiece. Good show!"

"I'm pleased, too, J. B.," the marketing director replied, "but not as pleased as I was last year 'cause Stick also seems to think that we won't make as much money on each subscription this time around."

"Izzat so, Stick?" the publisher asked. "How come?"

The controller cleared his throat and answered. "Well, Chief, you remember, don't you, that our contract with the union expires next year? It's going to be a tough negotiation this time. We got by last time without a pay hike because our profits looked so bad, but now that they're healthy again, the union wants its cut."

The publisher frowned. "What are the damages going to be, Stick?"

"As best I can tell, pay hikes probably will be in the range of 10 percent, which translates into a jump in costs of about $3 for the second year of each subscription," the controller said, "but exactly how much it'll be is anyone's guess. And that's on top of the big price increase our paper suppliers are laying on us for next year. I've had Purchasing calling around for better prices, but it looks like the suppliers are all going up the same as ours, so we're going to have to eat another $2 hit per subscription in the second year."

"Ouch!" the publisher complained. "Seems like whenever we get a little ahead, something jumps up and bites us in the ankle."

"My sentiments exactly, J. B.," the marketing director chimed in. "You couldn't have said it better."

* * * *

What liability (if any) for the new subscriptions should be recognized upon their receipt and at the end of the first of the two years?

THE NOTE RECEIVABLE CASE

"Can we take it at face value?"

Just as winter was beginning to set in, Charlie's Carpentry Company was able to finish framing and "drying-in" a new lake house for Frank Fisher, one of its clients, who accepted the work as complete and satisfactory. Fisher is building the lake house as a weekend and summer retreat for himself and his family on a lot he bought for $18,000 last spring with some inheritance money. To keep construction costs to a minimum, Fisher decided to be his own general contractor.

Although the lot is fully paid for, the house must be financed. Because local lending institutions do not make loans to individuals on dwellings that are not yet habitable, Fisher has had to work out some short-term financing arrangements. He has arranged with a building supply company to buy all the materials needed on a six-month note and has made a similar arrangement with Charlie's Carpentry for the labor. Now that the house is "dried-in," Fisher plans to spend his winter weekends doing all the finishing work so that the house will be ready for use by late spring. Once the lake house is complete, Fisher intends to get a conventional mortgage on it for about $25,000 and use the proceeds to pay the notes to the building supply company and Charlie's Carpentry.

The job required a total of 310 hours of labor, for which Charlie's Carpentry usually bills $30 per hour on a cash basis (the workers are paid an hourly rate of $20). However, because of Fisher's good credit rating, the company has agreed to take a non-interest-bearing note in the face amount of $10,000, due in 6 months. Collateral for the note is a lien on the lake property (the same as on the note to the building supply company). Based on inquiries to its own bank and a few others, Charlie's Carpentry knows the note can be discounted with recourse for about $9,100 or without recourse for about $8,400.

From its own experience with similar notes, Charlie's Carpentry believes the risk of loss from default is about 5 percent. Also, the company usually charges a 12 percent annual discount rate.

* * * *

How should Charlie's Carpentry recognize the note receivable and the related service revenue?

THE PAYABLE CASE

"Pay me now or pay me later"

Tim's Time-Tested Auto Parts deals in second-hand auto parts salvaged from wrecked and abandoned vehicles. Because all the parts are used, Tim's sells only on an "as-is" basis; no returns, refunds, exchanges, or credits are permitted.

His customers are largely individuals who have the skill and tools to repair their own automobiles and various "shade-tree mechanics" who do low-cost repairs for others (with minimal overhead) in competition with established repair shops. Because his inventory is so extensive, Tim's is widely recognized as "the place to go" in Hazard County to get hard-to-find parts.

Hazard County is not a particularly prosperous place, and many of Tim's customers tend to live from paycheck to paycheck. Thus, when their cars break down, they often lack the necessary cash in their pockets to pay for the bigger-ticket items like used engines and transmissions. To accommodate them, Tim's sells merchandise either for cash or short-term non-interest-bearing notes (to those meeting his credit standards). However, to encourage cash purchases, Tim's offers a 5 percent discount for cash. Short-term notes are all payable at the end of the month (which is payday for General Gravel, the county's largest employer).

Danny Duke, a local shade-tree mechanic, has just purchased a used transmission that he is going to install for Sally Mae, one of his customers. He has quoted her a total price of $550, $300 for parts and $250 for labor.

Sally Mae will not be able to pay Danny until she gets paid by General Gravel, at which time Danny will be able to pay Tim's. Accordingly, Tim's agreed to sell the transmission to Danny for $200 on a regular short-term note.

*   *   *   *

How should Danny Duke recognize the purchase?

THE PENALTY CLAUSE CASE

"Taking a hit"

The Beachfront Resort suffered extensive damage last fall as a result of Hurricane Hattie. Some of the beachside villas were completely destroyed, and the rest suffered extensive damage. The marina and the fleet of rental boats were a total loss. Only the hotel and casino were spared from damage. Fortunately, virtually everything was fully insured.

Ronald Grump, owner of the resort, has been scrambling to prepare for this year's tourist season. Insurance claims have been filed and collected. New boats and furniture have been ordered and received. Staff has been hired for the season, and an extensive advertising campaign has been mounted to assure tourists that Beachfront Resort will be open and ready for business by June 1, the beginning of the important summer season.

All reconstruction work on the villas and marina has been contracted out to Coastal Construction. Terms of the contract call for Coastal to supply all materials and labor and to take care of all necessary permits—in effect, a "turnkey" job. The total price agreed on was $4.2 million. Although Coastal assured him that the job would be done by May 31, Grump insisted on including a stiffer penalty clause in the contract than the typical one in Coastal's contracts, which provides for a penalty of $1,000 per day. After extensive negotiations, a penalty clause of $50,000 per day was settled on, an amount equal to what Beachfront Resort would lose in revenue for each day the job was late.

The job was completed 10 days late, and the $500,000 penalty was deducted from the total price, leaving $3.7 million, which was then paid to Coastal. Concerned about what the impact of losing 10 days of rentals would have on the income statement, Grump instructed his controller to book the penalty as "revenue earned in lieu of lost rental revenue."

* * * *

a. What entry would be necessary for Grump to recognize the penalty as revenue? What would be the justification for it?
b. How should Coastal recognize the penalty?
c. Assume that the contract also included an "incentive clause" that provided for an additional payment to Coastal of $20,000 per day if the job was completed early. If Coastal finished its work 10 days ahead of schedule, how should Grump recognize the additional payment? How should Coastal recognize it?

THE PENSION ENHANCEMENT CASE

"Sweetening the pot"

Faber College is a relatively small private university that was founded in the early 1900s. Originally known primarily as a party school, Faber is now generally regarded as one of the better colleges in its region.

From its founding, Faber has enjoyed strong financial support from the Faber family, as well as other benefactors, friends, and alumni; as a consequence, it is well endowed and its board of trustees has considerable resources at its command. Headed by its strong-willed multimillionaire chairperson, Edgar Hart Faber, the board has used those resources agressively to recruit highly talented students and faculty, as well as to upgrade and expand the physical plant. The board is strongly committed to achieving national recognition for Faber College and has funded a sizeable public relations department to publicize Faber's highly select student body, well-published faculty, and beautiful campus.

Faber was one of the first colleges to establish a pension plan for its faculty and staff. The original plan, established 50 years ago, was a defined benefit plan with retirement benefits based on the retiree's highest salary. That plan was replaced 15 years ago with a defined contribution plan, but all who retired under the original plan are still covered by it.

Inflation has steadily eroded the purchasing power of benefits paid under the original plan to the degree that retirees who must rely solely on plan benefits and social security to cover their living costs are finding it increasingly difficult to make ends meet. Two reports in the local newspapers about the difficulties Faber's retirees are facing have deeply troubled E. H. Faber and the board.

An emergency board meeting was called for the day after the reports appeared. Following the meeting, at a press conference hastily organized by Faber College's public relations department, E. H. Faber proudly announced that the board had voted to "double the benefits to our family of retirees, effective immediately, in order to recognize their many years of faithful service and their contributions to the ever-growing greatness that Faber College represents." The added benefits will cost Faber an average of about $500,000 per year for the next 10 years and have an actuarial present value of about $4 million.

* * * *

How should Faber College account for the enhancement of its retirees' benefits?

32

THE PETROLEUM CASE

"Oklahoma crude (and refined)"

Oilco is a regional oil company involved in exploration, production, refining, and marketing of oil and petroleum products (primarily gasoline). Oilco's primary oil reserves are located in Oklahoma. It has two refineries, one in Oklahoma near its reserves and the other in Indiana. Oilco markets its products through its own Oilco service stations (located primarily in the Midwest) and unbranded through several independent station chains.

Oilco's crude oil production of 200,000 barrels per day exceeds the combined capacities of its Oklahoma and Indiana refineries (80,000 and 50,000 barrels per day, respectively) to refine it into gasoline and other petroleum products. In addition, Oilco purchases crude oil for its Indiana refinery when the sales value of its Oklahoma crude plus transportation costs exceeds the price of crude available locally. As a consequence, more than half of Oilco's crude production is sold to other refiners.

About half of Oilco's refinery production of gasoline is sold through its own service stations, and the rest is sold to independents. Oilco continuously reviews gasoline availability and prices to determine whether to transport its own refined product to its stations or to sell it and purchase refined product for its stations locally. Those decisions primarily are based on local market prices and transportation costs. Oilco is not a big enough factor in the industry to influence the market; hence, the immediate sale of all its inventories would have an indiscernible effect on market prices.

*   *   *   *

Should Oilco recognize income on its inventories of crude oil and gasoline (i.e., "mark to [wholesale] market")?

THE PLUMBING CASE

"It's a lead pipe cinch"

The Reuss Corporation is a real estate developer. In addition to developing raw land, it constructs and rehabilitates office buildings, which it then sells.

Reuss recently acquired the building of a failed savings and loan company for $5 million. The building has been vacant since last year when the government declared the S&L to be insolvent and sold its assets to another, healthier one. Reuss bought the building with the intention of gutting much of the interior, remodeling it into a modern, "class A" office building, and then selling it.

Because the building was constructed a number of years ago, lead pipes were installed for its plumbing system. Because lead pipes have been found to contaminate the water they carry, the government has deemed them to be a health hazard and adopted regulations requiring their removal and replacement whenever a building is renovated. Reuss was aware of the regulation when negotiating for the building's purchase.

The total cost of remodeling the building will be $4 million, of which $500,000 is for removal of the lead pipes and replacement with copper plumbing. The remodeling will not increase the building's expected useful life, although it will enhance its rental value.

*   *   *   *

a. How should Reuss recognize the cost of removing and replacing the plumbing system?
b. Assuming Reuss was not aware of either the regulation or the presence of the lead pipes, how should it recognize the cost?

THE PRODUCTION RIGHTS CASE

"It's a deep subject"

J. R. Maverick's ranch is one of the biggest west of the Pecos River. Despite its size, however, it is one of the few with virtually no oil on it. The only operating well is on the north edge of the ranch, adjacent to one of the richest oil patches in the state of Texas.

Although the well is more than 20 years old, it is a consistent producer. Year in and year out, the well has produced 10,000 barrels of West Texas Intermediate Crude, the grade of oil used as a benchmark for oil pricing. Based on geologists' estimates of the well's remaining reserves, the well should be able to continue producing at that level for about 10 more years.

Over the well's life, oil prices at the wellhead have ranged from a low of $5 per barrel to nearly $40 per barrel. The most recent quotes have been about $20 per barrel, although prices have been as high as $22 and as low as $18 in the past year. Current lifting costs for the well are about $8 per barrel and are expected to remain at or near that level for the foreseeable future.

Shortly after reaching his 83d birthday, J. R. passed away. In his last will and testament, he bequeathed all rights to the well's production to his aged widow, Ima, for the next five years. After that, all rights are to go to his alma mater, Wheat University (a private institution).

*   *   *   *

How should Wheat University recognize the bequest of production rights?

THE PURCHASE-SALE COMMITMENT CASE

"Assets? Liabilities? Both? Neither?"

"As this company's purchasing agent, I'm tired of catching it from Finance for 'overbuying' when I think the market's weak and from Production for 'underbuying' when I think it's high," said Bob Byer. "I'll buy our entire next year's supply of exwyes from you if you'll give me a locked-in price."

"That's an attractive order," said Sarah Sellers, the supplier's sales manager, "and one I know we can fill. Here's my deal: a 1-year noncancellable contract for 10,000 exwyes per month at today's market of $5 apiece: deliveries to be made on the first of each month, with payment for each shipment within 30 days of delivery. Since neither of us can cancel, it's like you getting a call option on the exwyes in exchange for us getting a put option on them."

"Sounds fair enough to me," Byer replied. "Just out of curiosity, though, what would a similar call option without the attached put have cost me?"

"Our usual arrangement is to charge 5 percent of what the total contract price would have been if the customer had taken delivery. In this case, that would be $30,000."

"Ouch! That much, eh? OK, let's go with the noncancellable deal. The purchase order will be ready to sign when we get back from lunch."

* * * *

a. What, if anything, should Byer's company recognize as a result of the postluncheon signing?
b. What, if anything, should Sellers' company recognize as a result of the postluncheon signing?
c. Would the answers to (a) and (b) change if the terms of the contract allowed Byer's company to decide not to take the exwyes, but required it to pay a penalty of $25,000 for not taking them?

THE PURCHASE-SALE OPTION CASE (PART I)

"Beyer buys"

"I hear the Union Building is up for sale," said Beth Beyer.

"Yep," answered Carl Cellar. "You can have it today for a price that's a real steal—only $1,000,000. Want it?"

"Could be. Not today, but maybe sometime soon. Want to sell me a six-month option to buy at that figure?"

"Sure would, but with two conditions. One, no refund of the option fee if you don't exercise. Two, no applying it to the purchase price if you do. Six-month purchase option to purchase the Union for $1,000,000; option fee, $15,000 in cash."

"Come on, Cellar—$15,000 with those conditions? Ten thousand dollars is tops, and I'll write you a check here and now."

"OK, Beyer, you've got yourself an option."

*   *   *   *

a. Cellar must debit Cash, but what should he credit?
b. Beyer must credit Cash, but what should she debit?

THE PURCHASE-SALE OPTION CASE (PART II)

"Cashing in"

A month after she purchased the option from Cellar, Beth Beyer got a phone call from Ben Broecker, a local investor. "Heard you got an option on the Union Building. Interested in selling it?"

Beth thought for a moment. "Maybe, Ben. What kind of price did you have in mind?"

"Well, I know you paid Carl $10,000 for it. How's about $15,000? That's a quick 50 percent profit on a 1-month investment. Hard to beat that!"

Knowing Ben was a shrewd investor and not one to throw his money around very readily, Beth thought perhaps he might have the inside scoop on something. There had been rumors circulating for the past few weeks that some big corporation was considering locating a major new division in town. If that happened, the demand for existing commercial space would skyrocket. On the other hand, there had been similar rumors before, but nothing ever materialized. "I dunno, Ben," she said. "I've heard something big might be about to pop in town, and I'd like to have a piece of it. I don't think I could let you have it for less than $20,000."

"Ouch!" Ben replied. "You're pretty proud of that option, aren't you? Tell you what—let's split the difference, and I'll give you $17,500 for it. What do you say?"

"Make it $18,500 and you've got a deal."

"Deal. I'll bring you the check this afternoon."

* * * *

How should Beyer recognize the sale of her option?

THE PURCHASE-SALE OPTION CASE (PART III)

"Speak now or . . ."

Nearly five months after buying the option from Beth Beyer, Ben Broecker received a phone call from Cellar. "Remember your option on the Union Building?" Cellar began. "It expires at the close of business tomorrow."

"Is that so?" Broecker replied. "You don't think I had forgotten, do you?"

"So what are you gonna do about it? Do we have a deal, or do I put it back on the market?" asked Cellar. "You know the rumor going around that General National Corporation may be coming to town. If they do, commercial space like the Union will be selling like hotcakes!"

"Well, that may or may not be true. We've all heard that rumor—and a dozen or so like it before," Broecker responded.

"You betcha, but this time I've got a hunch it'll be the real thing. In fact, I feel so strongly about it that I'm not going to put the Union up for option again once yours expires," Cellar said.

Broecker thought for a moment. "Let me sleep on it overnight. I'll let you know tomorrow. OK?"

"Fine, but I'll need to know no later than 5 o'clock."

*　*　*　*

a. If Broecker exercised his option, what should be recognized?
b. If Broecker let the option lapse, what should be recognized?
c. Assume that Broecker also held a second option on a similar piece of property for which he had paid $20,000. The option price for the second property was $950,000. Although he intended only to purchase one piece of property, he had acquired both options in order to "buy time" to allow him to research which of the two properties would best suit his needs. If he exercised the second option and let this one lapse, how should the lapse be recognized?

THE RESTRICTED TICKET CASE

"Gladhand has reservations . . ."

Gib Gladhand, a New York City-based account sales executive for Titan Industrial Corporation, has been working hard to develop a new customer, Outback & Co., in Des Moines, Iowa. Agreement is nearly at hand on a major contract that will represent Titan's first in the Farm Belt, a region heretofore the exclusive province of its chief competitor, the Chicago Western Company.

For contract renewals and other repeat business, closings usually are done by mail, telephone, overnight letters, and FAX machines. However, because Gladhand hopes to generate additional business from Outback, he feels a more personal touch is in order and has decided to be present in Des Moines for the contract's final inking. Closing is planned to take place on either Tuesday or Friday of the first full week in January, depending on when the lawyers are able to finalize the details of the contract (Outback's president will be unavailable the rest of the week).

In view of Titan's belt-tightening efforts to control travel and entertainment expenses, Gladhand asked his secretary, Miss Farthing, to arrange for the lowest-cost air fare available. She learned that Super-Duper Fares are available for both the Tuesday and Friday dates. Being midweek, the Tuesday round-trip fare of $350 is somewhat higher than the Friday round-trip fare of $300. Both fares require immediate purchase, are not refundable, and carry a 100 percent cancellation penalty. The only other option is the regular round-trip coach fare of $900 that requires no advance purchase and carries no restrictions.

She decided to purchase Super-Duper Fares for both the Tuesday and Friday dates, reasoning that would save Titan $250 ($350 plus $300 as opposed to $900) and Gladhand simply could use whichever set of tickets was needed and discard the other. Pleased with her resourcefulness, Gladhand congratulated her for a job well done.

Bragging on his secretary's achievement to Titan's controller over lunch, Gladhand got an unexpectedly chilly response. Instead of being pleased about the cost savings, the controller was upset, asking, "How in Sam Hill do you expect us to book this?"

* * * *

How should Titan recognize on its year-end financial statements the two sets of tickets that were purchased?

THE SABBATICAL CASE

"The seven-year itch . . ."

Nipp & Tuck (N&T), a large national law firm, has provided continuing professional education (CPE) for its attorneys for years. Courses were taught internally by partners and staff who had both the interest and skills to teach.

The need for a permanent training facility became evident as the firm grew and an ideal facility, a former prep school, with classrooms, offices, a library, dining halls, and dormitories was found. After acquiring the facility, N&T began offering CPE training to outsiders on a "space available" basis in classes being taught for its own staff, charging fees to offset some of the costs of its own training. An untapped market for CPE clearly existed, for soon the firm was turning away more clients than it was able to serve.

To capitalize on that market, N&T decided to offer a whole range of additional CPE courses. Having exhausted its internal pool of instructional talent, N&T hired a cadre of experienced instructors to bring quickly an expanded program on line. To add credibility to its offerings, N&T offered professors from distinguished law schools compensation packages that were highly competitive with universities.

Among the benefits was a sabbatical leave program. N&T was aware that universities routinely provide faculty with leaves every seven years to "rebuild their intellectual capital." No duties are assigned them during the leaves, and they are free to spend the time however they wish. Leaves typically are for either a half-year at full pay or a full year at half-pay. To compensate for the lack of a tenure system, N&T offered leaves of one year at full pay after 7 years of service. No conditions are attached except that the instructors are expected to return for at least one year following the leave.

Shortly after joining the firm in December, the new office manager learned that Elwood Chipps, the first faculty member to become eligible for a leave, would begin his sabbatical on January 1. Chipps will be paid a salary of $150,000 during his sabbatical, and the office manager is wondering whether that amount should be charged to (1) past service, (2) future service, or (3) expense during the period of the sabbatical.

*   *   *   *

How should Nipp & Tuck recognize the cost of the sabbatical?

THE SICK PAY CASE

"Just take two aspirin . . ."

Goodhart's Gourmet, a small specialty food store, recently adopted a policy of compensating employees who are absent from work because of personal illness. Prior to adoption of the policy, all employees had their pay docked for any kind of absence from work, including being sick.

The policy applies only to full-time employees who have worked for the company for at least six months. Under the policy, employees are entitled to be paid at their regular pay rate for all days they are absent from work because of illness, subject to a maximum of the number of "sick days" accrued to date. Sick days accrue at the rate of one day per month that the employee has worked, beginning when the employee was hired. Thus, during the first six months of employment, an employee would receive no compensation for absences due to illness, but on the completion of six months of service the employee would have accrued six sick days that could be applied immediately to his or her next illness. Sick days accumulated can be carried forward without limit. However, upon termination of employment (either voluntary or involuntary), neither is "terminal leave" (that is, paid leave at the end of employment) permitted for sick days not taken, nor is any payment made for sick days not taken.

Alvin Ailing commenced employment at Goodhart's on January 1 of the current year and became eligible for sick pay on July 1. He is paid at the rate of $10 per hour, or $80 per 8-hour workday.

* * * *

a. What liability, if any, should Goodhart's recognize on its calendar-year financial statements for the sick days Alvin has accrued by year-end?
b. If Carol O'Chronic commenced work on September 1 at the same pay rate as Alvin, what liability, if any, should Goodhart's recognize at year-end for the sick days she has accrued?
c. If Goodhart's policy contained no prohibition against either terminal leave or payment upon termination for sick days accrued but not taken, would that change the answer to (a) above and, if so, how?

THE SILENT AUCTION CASE

"Pinchpenny gets the Goods . . ."

Each year, the Lilianne Orphanage holds a gala fund-raiser to help underwrite the institution's annual operating costs and to fund certain capital improvements. This year, a new feature was added to the fund-raiser, a "silent auction," in which items auctioned off included a wide array of goods and services contributed by local businesses and professionals.

One of the items contributed was the preparation of an individual's federal income tax return (Form 1040). The contributor was Albee Good, a young CPA who, in partnership with her sister, opened a public accounting practice in town a few years ago. The firm's client base has grown steadily, and by any measure the firm of Good & Good would be regarded as quite successful.

In the firm, the typical 1040 is billed out at $400, an amount that reflects the staff time required to prepare the return (6 hours at $40 per hour) as well as the time of 1 of the 2 partners to conduct the initial client interview and to review and sign the return (2 hours at $80 per hour). Partners are not paid salaries per se, but rather they share in the firm's profits. For the past couple of years, profits to the partners, divided by the number of hours they work annually, have averaged about $50 an hour.

The person who submitted the winning bid of $500 was James Cash Pinchpenny, the town's wealthiest man. For the past several years, Pinchpenny has had his personal tax return prepared by a large public accounting firm in nearby Metropolis City. Because of the complexity of his return, he has been charged about $4,000 per year for his return.

*   *   *   *

a. Should Good & Good recognize a liability to Pinchpenny and, if so, in what amount? Also, what account should be debited?
b. Should Pinchpenny recognize an asset and, if so, in what amount? Also, what account should be credited?

43

THE SMOKESTACK CASE

"Blowing smoke"

Industrial Iron Works is a classic example of a "smokestack company." It is in a declining industry that has been beset by foreign competition. Moreover, the industry is regarded as a "dirty" one that is being heavily impacted by new environmental regulations. Because its profits are already only marginal, Industrial is having difficulty affording the costs of complying with those regulations.

Industrial is located in the middle-sized community of Hidden Valley, so named because of its location in a picturesque valley. Industrial is one of only two significant employers in the city, the other being Valley Electronics, a specialist in producing electronic subassemblies for use in computers.

Valley Electronics is almost the direct opposite of Industrial. It is in a "clean" industry that has been growing rapidly and is highly profitable. The biggest problem Valley faces is being able to attract qualified employees to staff its expansion. Prospective employees have been turned off by the air pollution created by Industrial that gets trapped in the valley.

The problem can be largely solved by the installation of "scrubbers" on Industrial's smokestacks, but the $3 million price tag is too great for Industrial to absorb. If forced to do so, it would have to close down its facility, turning hundreds out of work.

To address the problem, Valley Electronics and the city of Hidden Valley have proposed sharing the $3 million cost equally, each picking up one-third. Industrial immediately accepted the offer. Installation of the scrubbers will not extend the iron works' expected life, efficiency, or capacity.

*   *   *   *

a. How should Industrial recognize the installation of the scrubbers?
b. How should Valley recognize its share of the cost?

THE STOCK INVESTMENT CASE

"Holding on"

Using some inheritance money, Larry Leisure bought 1,000 shares of stock in Leisure Products Corporation at market price 5 years ago. The company had been founded by Larry's great grandfather and had grown to such a size that its shares were publicly traded on a regional stock exchange when Larry bought them. One-hundred-thousand shares were authorized, issued, and outstanding, and the shares were trading for $50 each at the time.

Shortly after he acquired the shares, the company went private, with all stockholdings being held by various members of the Leisure family. No shares have changed hands since the company went private, nor have any additional shares been authorized or issued.

Larry has continued to hold the shares as an investment, using the quarterly dividends to supplement his earnings as a part-time ski instructor and busboy. He also views the shares as reserve against any future cash needs he might have.

In the 5 years since Larry became a stockholder, both earnings and dividends on the stock have risen by one-third, from $6 and $3 per share to $8 and $4, respectively. During that same period, prices of stocks of all publicly traded companies have risen by 25 percent, on average, and the Consumer Price Index has climbed 20 percent.

Larry has not given much thought to selling his shares, but since receiving an unsolicited cash offer from his sister to buy all of his shares at $65 each, he has been thinking about it.

Perplexed, he has asked his accountant, Bev Booker, to prepare a set of personal financial statements for him, reasoning that she will need to ascertain a sound measure of his holdings for the statements.

* * * *

a. How should Bev recognize Larry's stockholding on the financial statements?
b. Assuming that Larry's company, Slipperyslope Ski School, had purchased the shares rather than Larry personally, should the stockholding be recognized differently on its financial statements than on Larry's personal financial statements? If so, why?

THE SWEAT EQUITY CASE

"Sweating it out"

Frank and Jesse are brothers. Frank, a carpenter, found a house commonly referred to in the real estate business as a "re-do" and brought it to the attention of Jesse, an investor. Although the house was structurally sound, it needed a considerable amount of remodeling and cosmetic work that Frank could do himself, working evenings and weekends over the course of a year. Because the house could be bought at the distressed price of $100,000, Frank convinced Jesse of the opportunity for making a significant profit by fixing it up. Based on present prices of comparable houses in good condition, the brothers expected to be able to sell the redone house for around $200,000.

The brothers worked out the following agreement. Jesse would provide all the financing through his company, Jesse's Investments. In turn, Frank would provide the labor through his company, Frank's Construction, in return for "sweat equity" in the house. Once the house was finished, either of two options would be available. One was to sell it, using the proceeds to pay off the loan and interest from Jesse's Investments, as well as repay it for the materials, and split the remainder equally. The other was for Frank's Construction to buy the house, paying off Jesse's Investments' share with the proceeds of a conventional mortgage based on the (redone) house's fair market value.

Jesse's Investments arranged to borrow the $100,000 needed to buy the house on a 1-year note bearing 10 percent interest, and also advanced the $10,000 needed for materials. Frank's Construction provided all the labor necessary to bring it to a "like-new" marketable condition, finishing the work on schedule.

As soon as the house was finished, the brothers obtained competent appraisals that indicated the fair market value of the redone house was $200,000. Frank's Construction then bought the house, taking out an 80 percent mortgage ($160,000) and using the proceeds as previously agreed.

* * * *

a. How should Frank's Construction recognize the purchase of the house?
b. Assuming instead that Frank's Construction took out a 90 percent mortgage, how should it recognize the purchase?

THE TOXIC DUMP CASE

"Cleaning up their act"

The Toxic Transport and Disposal Company (TTD) is in the business of picking up and hauling away the hazardous wastes that are created as byproducts of various manufacturing companies. The wastes are taken to any one of several of the company's toxic dump sites, depending on the nature of the waste and the location of the pick-up point.

One of the dump sites TTD operates is in the small community of Sour Lake. That site is the company's oldest and, at one time, received all nature of waste. Some of the earliest waste was buried in steel drums that have developed leaks over the years. As a consequence of those leaks, hazardous substances have contaminated the soil.

To address that problem, TTD plans to refine the soil and install a liner at the dump. Soil refinement will return the soil to a condition approximating what it was originally before the site was used as a dump. The liner will prevent future soil contamination from occurring. Refinement of the soil is expected to cost $500,000 and installation of the liner, $800,000.

* * * *

a. Assuming the dump site is to continue in operation, how should the costs of refining the soil and installing the liner be recognized?
b. Assuming the dump site is to be permanently closed, how should the costs be recognized?

THE VENTURE CASE

"Taking a flier . . ."

I. N. Trepid, an entrepreneur, is what might be termed a "charter broker." In that capacity, Trepid engages in individual ventures in which he charters a jetliner, complete with crew, to fly to various resort destinations and sells seats on that flight to individual passengers.

For his current venture, he has chartered a 300-seat jetliner to fly from New York to Florida. This charter contract with the airline company calls for a charter fee of $10,000 to make that flight, payable on departure. However, the contract permits him to cancel the contract at any time up to 10 days prior to departure by paying a $3,000 penalty. If the airline company fails to provide the aircraft and crew as promised, it must arrange for alternative transportation on the same day for each ticketed passenger, either by scheduled flights or other charters. Otherwise, the airline must refund to each passenger all monies paid, plus a 50 percent penalty.

For competitive reasons, the entrepreneur has decided to sell each seat on the flight at the bargain price of $100, payable in full when the seat is purchased. The ticket is refundable by the broker only in the event he cancels the flight.

The break-even point for this venture is 100 passengers; above that, it will make a profit and below that, a loss. With fewer than 70 tickets sold, cancelling the flight would result in a small loss. Trepid has had to cancel about 25 percent of previous charters to this destination and, because the pattern of ticket sales is irregular, a "go" or "no-go" decision cannot be readily predicted.

* * * *

a. What are the broker's liabilities 1 month prior to departure with:
    50 tickets sold?
    80 tickets sold?
    150 tickets sold?
b. What are the broker's liabilities 1 week prior to departure with:
    50 tickets sold?
    80 tickets sold?
    150 tickets sold?